Prehistoric
Record Breakers

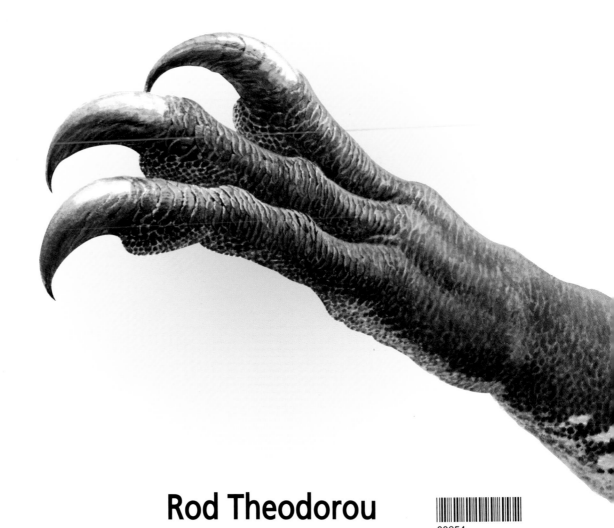

Rod Theodorou

Acknowledgements

Photos
Rupert Horrox, photography, pages 4, 11, 17, 20 and 21. Bruce Coleman
Limited/Hans Reinhard, page 7. J Allan Cash Limited, page 9. Dr Alan
Beaumont, page 13. Ardea/Clem Haagner, page 19. Bruce Coleman
Limited/Uwe Walz, page 22.

Thanks to St Mary and John CE First School, Oxford, for use of a wooden
meter rule.

Illustrations
James Field/Simon Girling Associates, pages 2, 5, 7, 9, 11, 15, 17, 19, 24 and
cover. Andrew Hutchinson/Illustration, pages 1, 4, 13, 20, 21, 22, 23.
Oxford Illustrators, pages 6, 8, 10, 12, 14, 16, 18

Heinemann Educational Publishers
Halley Court, Jordan Hill, Oxford OX2 8EJ
a division of Reed Educational & Professional Publishing Ltd

OXFORD   MELBOURNE   AUCKLAND
JOHANNESBURG   BLANTYRE   GABORONE
IBADAN   PORTSMOUTH (NH) USA   CHICAGO

© Reed Educational & Professional Publishing Ltd 1997

First published 1997

02 01 00 99 98

10 9 8 7 6 5

British Library Cataloguing in Publication Data
A catalogue record for this book is available from the British Library.

ISBN 0 435 09565 X   *Prehistoric Record Breakers* individual copy pack:
                                        6 copies of 1 title

ISBN 0 435 09416 5   Stage F pack: 1 each of 7 titles

Colour reproduction by Reacta Graphics.

Printed and bound in Great Britain by Scotprint.

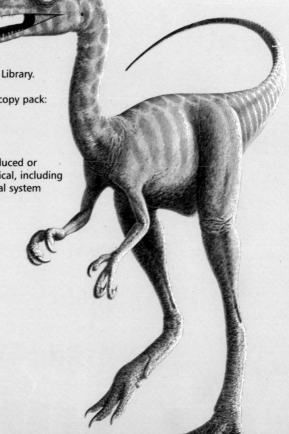

Contents

About this book

Prehistoric animals died millions of years ago. Prehistoric animals included dinosaurs, reptiles and insects.

Have you ever wondered what they were like?

In this book you will find

- information about some of the record-breaking prehistoric animals

- pictures of what these prehistoric animals might have looked like

- guides to help you pronounce each prehistoric animal name

- measurements and scale diagrams of the prehistoric animals

Smallest dinosaur

Name: Compsognathus

Pronounced: Komp-sog-nay-thus

Size: 75 centimetres long

Compsognathus is the smallest dinosaur ever to have been discovered. It was a meat-eater. It had long legs and could run fast. This helped it to catch lizards and insects to eat.

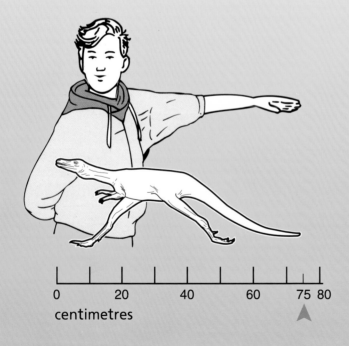

0   20   40   60   75 80
centimetres

Compsognathus was about the size of a chicken.

Largest dinosaur

Name: Argentinosaurus

Pronounced: Ah-jen-teen-oh-sore-us

Size: 33.5 metres long

Some scientists think that Argentinosaurus is the largest and heaviest dinosaur ever to have been discovered. Only a few bones of this massive plant-eater have been found. Argentinosaurus may have weighed more than 12 elephants!

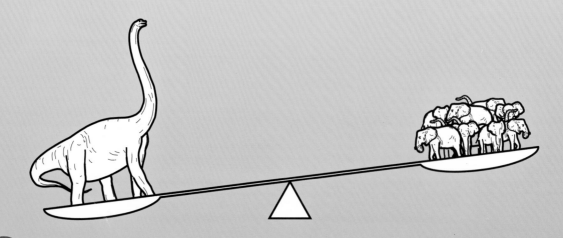

Argentinosaurus was as large as a three storey building.

Largest meat-eating dinosaur

Name: Giganotosaurus

Pronounced: Jie-gan-oh-toh-sore-us

Size: 13.5 metres long

Giganotosaurus is the biggest meat-eating land animal ever to have lived. This predator was even bigger than Tyrannosaurus rex! It was as long as four cars.

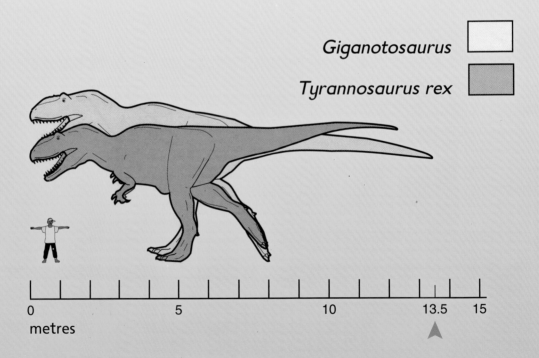

Giganotosaurus

Tyrannosaurus rex

0   5   10   13.5   15

metres

Giganotosaurus had teeth
15 centimetres long!

Largest flying reptile

- **Name:** Quetzalcoatlus
- **Pronounced:** Kwet-zal-co-art-lus
- **Size:** 12 metre wingspan

Quetzalcoatlus is the largest flying creature ever to have lived. Its head was bigger than a whole person! Some scientists think it lived like a giant vulture, eating the bodies of dead dinosaurs.

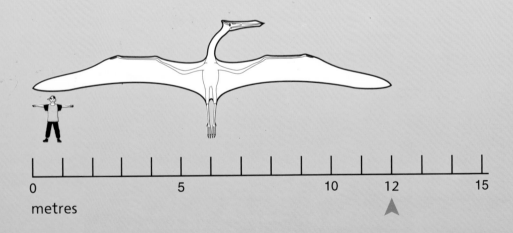

0   5   10   12   15

metres

The wingspan of Quetzalcoatlus was longer than the wingspan of a small plane!

Largest marine reptile

Name: Kronosaurus

Pronounced: Kron-oh-sore-us

Size: Over 15 metres long

Kronosaurus is the largest marine or swimming reptile ever to have been discovered. Its head was twice the length of Giganotosaurus' head. Inside its huge mouth were 80 massive teeth. It used these to crush giant turtles and other prey.

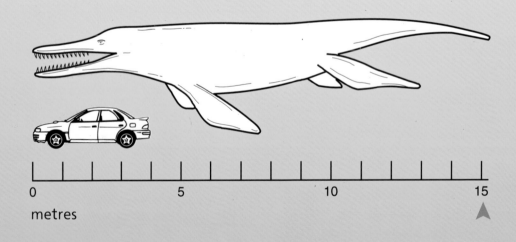

0				5				10				15

metres

Kronosaurus was as big as a whale.

Largest insect

- **Name:** Meganeura
- **Pronounced:** Meg-ah-new-ra
- **Size:** 70 centimetre wingspan

Meganeura is the largest insect ever to have lived. It was a huge dragonfly that hunted other large insects and small lizards. It may have hovered just like dragonflies do today.

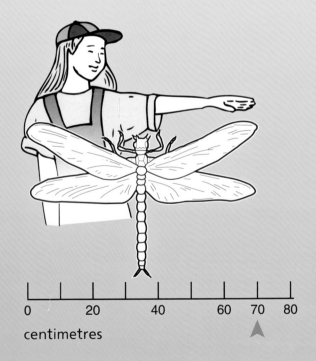

0   20   40   60 70 80

centimetres

Meganeura must have made a
very loud buzzing noise as it flew!

Fastest dinosaur

- **Name:** Struthiomimus

- **Pronounced:** Strew-thee-oh-mie-mus

- **Speed:** About 70 kilometres an hour

Many scientists think Struthiomimus was the fastest dinosaur ever to have lived. It had big, strong legs with huge muscles. These helped it to run away from predators. It ate leaves, insects and small animals.

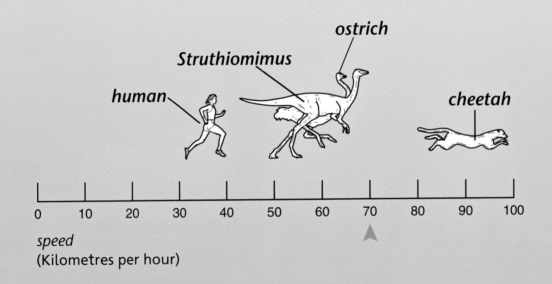

speed
(Kilometres per hour)

Struthiomimus looked like an ostrich but was probably a faster runner.

Longest arms

 **Name:** Deinocheirus

 **Pronounced:** Dine-oh-kire-us

 **Arm size:** Over 4 metres long

Deinocheirus had the longest arms of any dinosaur. We do not know what Deinocheirus looked like because only the fossil arm bones have been found. They were five times longer than an adult human's arm!

Deinocheirus must have been a huge predator!

Largest claws

- **Name:** Therizinosaurus
- **Pronounced:** Theh-ree-zin-oh-sore-us
- **Claw size:** Over 90 centimetres long

Therizinosaurus had the largest claws of any dinosaur. Only the fossil claws and a few other small bones have been found. Some scientists think that the large claws were used to dig into termite hills.

Therizinosaurus had claws longer than an adult human's leg.

Largest head

- **Name:** Torosaurus

- **Pronounced:** Tor-oh-sore-us

- **Head size:** Over 3 metres long

Torosaurus had the largest head of any land animal ever to have lived. It was about as long as a family car! It may have used its huge head and sharp horns to scare off enemies.

Torosaurus had a head as big as a whole rhino!

Glossary

fossil

the remains of a living thing that has turned to stone

predator

an animal that hunts and eats other animals

prey

an animal that is hunted and eaten by other animals

scale diagram

a drawing that shows the size of something

wingspan

the length of an animal from the tip of one wing to the tip of the other wing

Index